www.booksbyboxer.com

Bee Three Publishing is an imprint of Books By Boxer
Published by
Books By Boxer, Leeds, LS13 4BS UK
Books by Boxer (EU), Dublin D02 P593 IRELAND
© Books By Boxer 2024
All Rights Reserved
MADE IN CHINA
ISBN: 9781915410344

This book is produced from responsibly sourced paper to ensure forest management

COOKING FOR ONE

RECIPES AND HACKS

From overcooking and wasting produce to feeling like all of the prep isn't worth it, cooking for one can have its drawbacks!

With these recipes and tips, you can make the most out of cooking for yourself again! From easy recipes perfect for a single portion, to tips and tricks to avoid food waste, save yourself some money when cooking for one. You can soon realize that cheffing it up doesn't necessitate a large group!

LOADED VEGGIE
FLATBREAD

A great way to have a quick, easy and delicious (cheat's) flatbread is by utilizing ready-made ingredients!

Store-bought flatbread, topped with some roasted vegetables, pesto, and cheese is a brilliant, quick and cheap combination!

What You'll Need:

Pre-made flatbread
Vegetables
Pesto or chutney
Cheese

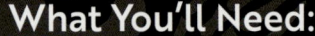

This is an easy and delicious recipe you can personalize, so is great for using up whatever you have in your cupboards and refrigerator!

1. Pre-roast some seasoned vegetables at a medium-high temperature for 30 minutes, or until charred. We recommend bell peppers, carrots, red onion, and zucchini, sprinkled with paprika, garlic powder, herb mix, salt, and pepper!

2. Bake your flatbread at the temperature on the packet. With 5 minutes to go, remove your flatbread and top with vegetables, some pesto (or chutney), and some left over cheese (cheddar, feta, parmesan and mozzarella are all great, but use your favorite!)

3. Once baked and crisp, slice up and serve with some salad!

TUNA PITTA POCKETS

Perfect for a mid-week quick dinner, or for a lunch to save you money, this super easy recipe is a great hack and makes a perfect single portion!

What You'll Need:

Pitta bread
1 can of tuna
Lettuce
Lemon juice
Cucumber
Red onion
(Other fresh salad items will work well!)

1. Shred lettuce and finely chop cucumber and some red onion. Add to a bowl with a squeeze of lemon and a pinch of fresh mint or parsley, and combine with tuna, salt, and pepper to taste.

2. Lightly toast your pitta bread until it puffs up slightly, and slice in half.

3. Stuff your pitta with the tuna salad and enjoy!

STUFFED
PEPPERS

Stuffed peppers are the ideal dish to make when you are cooking for one, simply make as many as you want to eat!

They are quick and easy, and can be made using pre-made ingredients to speed up the process!

What You'll Need:

Bell peppers
1 pouch of pre-cooked rice or cous cous
(Choose your favorite flavor!)
Fresh tomatoes
Cheese
(We love goat's cheese or mozzarella, but any cheese works well!)

1. Cook your cous cous or rice as per your packet instructions and season well to preference.

2. Slice the peppers in half and microwave for around 5 minutes, until slightly softened.

3. While they are cooking, combine your grain of choice with the sliced fresh tomatoes and cheese. Season with salt and pepper (add some pesto too, if you some to hand!)

4. Add the filling to your peppers, and then top with some extra cheese and bake in the oven on a medium-high temperature for 5 - 10 minutes, until the cheese has melted.

EASY
YAKISOBA

Utilizing your favorite ramen noodle packet in an elevated way is great for a one-man-meal!

What You'll Need:

1 packet of your favorite ramen noodles
Spring onions
Grated carrot
Bell peppers
Cabbage
Eggs

(This recipe works well with any vegetables you like or need to use up, so get creative!)

1. Cook your noodles as per the packet instructions, leaving the flavor packet out.

2. While they are cooking, fry up your vegetables in some oil and soy sauce. Add some ginger or garlic for an extra punch!

3. Once the noodles are cooked, drain and add to your vegetable pan, before adding the flavor packet! Stir well and cook for 1-2 minutes.

4. Serve with a fried egg and some hot sauce and enjoy!

BAKED
POTATO

A baked potato is one of life's comfort meals, and is an easy and filling dinner for when you are cooking for one!

The best thing about a good baked potato, is you can fill it with any filling you choose and it will (probably) still taste delicious!

You can cook a baked potato in multiple ways, but we recommend piercing the potato and microwaving for around 7-10 minutes, flipping halfway.

Once fork tender, spray with oil and transfer to a hot oven for a further 10 minutes, or until the skin is crisp (unless you're feeling lazy, then eat it straight from the microwave!)

Stuff your baked potato with butter and cheese to keep things simple or try these fillings:
Sour cream and chives
Leftover chili con carne or bolognese
Curry
Pesto, tomato and mozzarella

STEAK & FRIES

When the steaks are high, give your 'taters a fry with this delicious recipe!

What You'll Need:

2 large potatoes (Maris Piper work best)
220g | 8oz sirloin steak
Vegetable oil
Dijon mustard
Ground salt and pepper

Peel the potatoes and cut into slices. Wash in cold water and dry with a kitchen towel. Heat vegetable oil in a fryer or suitable pan to 140 - 160°C/280 - 320°F and cook the fries until golden.

Heat a griddle pan with 1 tsp. oil over high heat, then add the steak and season lightly with salt and pepper.

Flipping halfway, cook for:
4 minutes = rare
6 minutes = medium
8 minutes = well done

Once cooked, allow to rest for a couple of minutes, then serve with a dash of Dijon mustard!

BUY IN BULK

One of the main ways to reduce waste and save money when you are cooking for one is to buy in bulk! Generally, whilst you may spend more initially, you will save more by having your ingredients stretching further.

Utilize your freezer and ensure to wrap things individually to make cooking with them easy.

Individually wrapping and freezing chicken breast, fish filets and other meats in single portions is a great way to limit food waste and help your groceries stretch!

Buying large packets of rice, pasta, and other ingredients that have a very long shelf life is also a great way to save some money in the long run!

If you find that you are likely to cook with vegetables more than eat them fresh, pre-chopping and freezing things like bell peppers, onions, garlic, carrot, mushrooms and other vegetables will stop them going bad and help you create delicious meals in no time!

OVERLAP INGREDIENTS *TO AVOID* WASTE

Another way to help you save some money when cooking for one is to meal plan (if you can), and choose things that have overlapping ingredients to prevent over-buying and wasting food!

Having staple ingredients that pack a punch, such as chili, onion, and garlic are a great place to start, then think about which vegetables are the most versatile and you can do the most with!

Bell peppers are popular in both asian and south american cooking whereas prawns and chicken work perfectly in pasta dishes and thai-style broths, so think about how you can utilise the same ingredient in different ways to get the most bang out of your buck!

If you don't want to plan ahead, and find yourself being more spontaneous when it comes to cooking, then consider core ingredients, such as potatoes, tinned tomatoes, some herbs and spices, grains, protein and neutral vegetables that can find a delicious home in a variety of meals, and get creative!

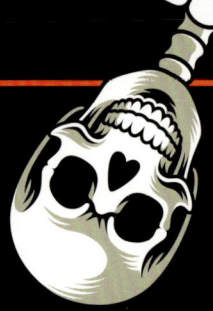

THE FREEZER
IS YOUR
FRIEND

Remember that the freezer is definitely your friend when it comes to cooking for one person! Whilst it's great to find recipes that are designed as meals for one, sometimes remember you can cook in batches and freeze for future use.

This can also help you save time in future, and stops you from spending hours each night making food!

Pies, soups, curries, broths and pasta dishes are all great for freezing! So think: if you are making a lasagne for one, make a big one and freeze it for future easy, delicious meals!

(Pre-portion your food into smaller containers, as you don't want to defrost the whole thing just to get a small piece!)

MICROWAVE MEALS

RECIPES AND HACKS

When cooking on a budget, you may find that you have one best friend to help you cook quickly, with little mess or without even needing to use the oven or gas at all: the trusty microwave.

From quick dinners that cook in minutes, to some handy hacks to help you use the microwave and up your cheffing game (even the professionals use it!), these recipes and tips are designed to help make your life easy!

VEGGIE
CHILI

Vegetables? Cheap. Powering a microwave? Quick. What more could a brokey like you want?! This recipe is a covenient and delicious answer to your broke but hungry prayers!

What You'll Need:

½ onion (chopped)
1 garlic clove (crushed)
Knob of butter
Pinch of chili powder
½ tsp. paprika
½ tsp. ground cumin
1 can chopped tomatoes (drained - reserve juice)
1 can kidney beans (drained)
½ veggie stock cube
2 squares of dark chocolate

1. Add garlic, onion, spices and butter into a microwavable bowl, stir and in the microwave, cook on high for 40 seconds. Add chopped tomatoes, chocolate, kidney beans, and stock cube, then stir.

2. Cover with cling film, pierce a few times and cook on high for 2 minutes (place kitchen paper underneath to catch spillages). Stir well.

3. Add a dash of saved tomato juice if the chili begins to dry out, then cover and cook for 2 minutes on medium, stir, and serve!

4. Why not garnish with a dollop of sour cream and coriander?

MAC &
CHEESE

Mac and cheese? Easy peasy!

What You'll Need:

Pasta
Milk
Butter
Cheese

1. Fill a microwavable mug halfway with pasta, then add 250ml | 8.45fl oz milk (or water/chicken stock if preferred). Cover with cling film and pierce a few times.

2. Stand the mug in a microwavable bowl (to catch spillages) in the microwave and cook on high for 2 minutes. Tip any spilled liquid back into the mug and stir. Then repeat twice (or until pasta feels cooked).

3. Add 2tsp. butter and a good portion of leftover cheese and sir well, then enjoy!

4. Why not add a dash of hot sauce or spinach to dress your mac and cheese?

RED LENTIL
DHAL

Making a meal is no big Dhal!

What You'll Need:

50g | ¼ cup red lentils
1 can chopped tomatoes
2 tsp. tikka curry paste

1. Using a colander, rinse the lentils well, then put into a microwavable bowl and add chopped tomatoes, tikka paste and 200ml/6¾oz water, before stirring.

2. Cover with a plate, then cook on high heat for 10 minutes, stir, re-cover, then cook for another 5 minutes.

3. Dish this out into a bowl, and serve!

Try making this meal even more delicious, by topping with natural yogurt and cilantro!

MUG
OMELETTE

Who said you need plates to make a meal?
Go gourmet with this meal in a mug!

1. Put a little butter into a microwavable mug and cook for 30 seconds, then stir. Swish the butter around the mug to coat the sides.

2. In a jug, beat 2 eggs and sprinkle a little salt and pepper into the mix, before adding in any little extras you fancy (parsley, peppers, shallots, cheese...)

3. Pour the mixture into the mug and cook for 60 seconds, stirring after every 20 seconds. Let the mug stand for a minute before eating.

CHOCOLATE
MUG
CAKE

Fancy dessert without the effort?

What You'll Need:

Self-raising flour
Caster sugar
Cocoa powder
Milk
1 egg
Oil (vegetable or sunflower)
Vanilla essence

1. In a jug, add 4 tbsp. flour, 4 tbsp. sugar, and 2 tbsp. cocoa powder and mix, then add an egg and mix again.

2. Add 3 tbsp. milk, 3 tbsp. oil, and a few drops vanilla essence then mix until smooth.

3. Pour the mixture into a microwavable mug, then cook on high for 1 ½ to 2 minutes (or until firm to the touch)

Why not swap out the essence to another flavor and add chocolate chips or nuts for an extra treat?

GARLICKY GREEN VEGETABLES

Get your microwave humming with these lean, mean, garlicky greens!

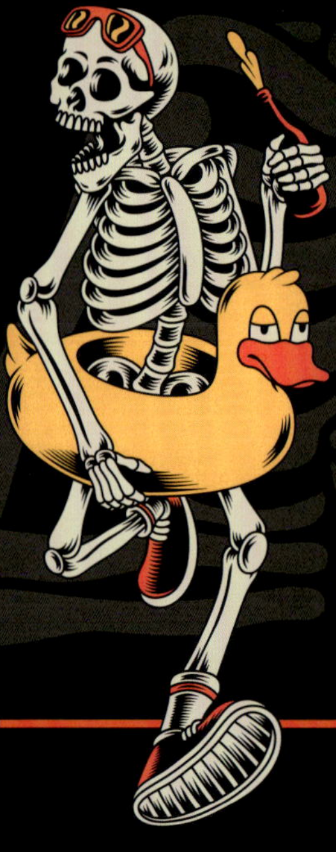

What You'll Need:

1 tbsp. olive oil
1 garlic clove (minced)
¼ tsp. chili flakes
Mixed green vegetables
(Broccoli, kale, asparagus
green beans etc.)

Add olive oil, chili flakes, garlic, and a pinch of salt and pepper into a microwavable bowl, cover, and cook for 1-2 minutes (until garlic is fragrant).

Then add your greens to the bowl, stir through, then cover and cook for 3 minutes or until the vegetables are tender.

These vegetables make a great side to most dishes!

ONION AND GARLIC IN THE
MICROWAVE

The microwave might seem like it isn't the answer to helping you along your culinary journey as a broke chef, but it can actually help you along, especially when dealing with delicious, staple ingredients that are a pain to prep!

1. REDUCE TEARS WHEN CUTTING ONION

If you find that you always cry when cutting onions, and this actually puts you off chopping them in the first place, try microwaving it! Placing the whole onion in the microwave for 30-45 seconds can break down the chemicals that cause you to cry!

2. EASY PEELERS

The struggle of peeling individual garlic cloves for a recipe can be really tedious, so why not try saving some time with this hack! Pop a whole garlic bulb in the microwave for around 20 seconds to lightly soften the cloves. This will mean they should slide out with ease!

REVIVE
OLD FOOD

Revive your stale bread with only a damp kitchen towel and a microwave! Just wrap the loaf in the damp towel and heat for 10 seconds - Now it's as fresh as the day you bought it!

Add crystallized honey into a microwave-safe container and heat on medium power for 30 seconds at a time, stirring inbetween (what a sweet trick!)

Make your soft nuts crunchy again, by roasting them! Spread them evenly on a microwavable plate, then blast on high for 1 minute intervals, between 3-8 minutes (depending on your nut of choice).

BANANA
PUDDING

Oh no! The folks are visiting and you have no idea what to serve them – don't worry! Try this microwave banana pudding that only takes 20 minutes and will use up some leftover bananas.

What You'll Need:

2 ripe bananas
2 eggs
¾ cup | 100g unsalted butter
¾ cup | 90g self-raising flour
⅓ cup | 90g light brown sugar
2 tbsp. milk of your choice

1. Put the butter in a large baking dish and microwave until melted for 30-60 seconds on high.

2. Mash the banana and add to the melted butter with the rest of the ingredients.

3. Mix all ingredients very well and cook for a further 8 minutes on high in the microwave.

4. The pudding should have cooked thoroughly and rise. Serve straight away while still warm.

QUICK
PICKLE

Pickles are delicious, and go with pretty much anything! Perfect to snack on, or to use up some extra vegetables in the fridge, a quick pickle is a great way to elevate any meal - and if you don't have enough time to wait, your trusty microwave can give you pickles in minutes!

Items that pickle well:

Cucumber
Onion / shallot
Cabbage
Chili
Radish
Green beans

Simply combine equal parts hot water and white vinegar, and season with salt and sugar to taste. You can add some extras such as peppercorns and garlic too!

We recommend using 1 cup water and 1 cup vinegar to 2 tsp. sugar and 2 tsp. salt, for a balanced pickling liquid!

Then, thinly slice your vegetables and add them to the liquid. Microwave for around 1 minute, stirring halfway.

These pickles will be lightly pickled and still have crunch, but can now be used in your dish! These work great as a side for tacos, in a sandwich, as a ramen topping or simply to munch on!

FREEZER FOOD

RECIPES AND HACKS

Don't let time get in the way of good food - fill your freezer and freeze the cost of your food shop! These recipes will keep you going day after day!

POMODORO
SAUCE

Perfect for dipping, making delicious pasta dishes, or using in sandwiches and on pizza, a good pomodoro sauce is a kitchen essential, and is essentially just a fancy tomato sauce.

It is a great base to help you elevate your food, and making it in bulk will help you to save some money!

This recipe is great to make in bulk, simply increase the ingredients proportionally! Freeze in individual portions and save the delicious sauce for when you really can't be bothered!

The trick to a good sauce is good ingredients. Think short term loss for long term gain... try to find good quality tinned tomatoes.

This is the first step, and pretty much the only thing you might need to splurge on (trust us, it's worth it). Then, for every tin of tomatoes, you will need around 3 cloves of garlic and 1/2 a white onion... simple really!

1. Dice your onion finely and cook in olive oil until transluscent.

2. Add your garlic and cook for around 2 minutes. (If you like it hot, add 1 tsp. red chili flakes in at this stage too).

3. Add your tomatoes, a generous pinch of salt and 1 tsp. of sugar. Season to taste!

4. If you have them available, add 1 bay leaf and cover. Allow to simmer for around 45 minutes on a low heat.

FLAVOR
BOMBS

Flavor bombs are a great way to preserve and make use of herbs before they go to waste.

What You'll Need:

1 icecube tray
1 garlic clove (crushed)
Fresh herbs (whatever you have laying around)
Olive oil

You can use these frozen flavor bombs whenever you want to add a splash of taste to your meal!

Fill each cube in the tray halfway with chopped fresh herbs. add 1tsp. garlic over the top and then fill the rest with olive oil.

Place in the freezer overnight, then transfer the frozen cubes into a freezer bag. Once frozen, these flavor bombs will last 4-6 months!

Our favorite combinations are:

Ginger, Chili, Garlic, Onion, Coriander (cilantro)
- Great for curries and Thai food!

Basil, Parsley, Chives, Garlic, Olive Oil
- Perfect to add a herby kick to Italian and Mediterranean dishes.

Garlic, Onion, Miso Paste, Sesame Oil, Soy Sauce
- Great to add to ramen noodles!

Garlic, Chili, Onion, Coriander, Tomato, Lime Juice
- Perfect for adding some zing to Mexican food!

LEEK & POTATO *SOUP*

Potato and leek to last through the week!

What You'll Need:

3 potatoes (peeled, cubed)
700ml | 3 cups veggie stock
200ml | 1 cup water
2 leeks (chopped)
2 tbsp. olive oil

1. Over medium heat, warm olive oil then add leeks and cook until soft, stirring frequently.

2. Add potatoes, water, stock and a pinch of salt, and bring to the boil before simmering for 20 minutes.

3. Add soup to a blender, and mix until smooth (this will make the soup taste better after freezing then reheating).

This recipe makes 6 servings.

EASY CHICKEN
AND PEA
RISOTTO

Don't *risotto* extreme measures,
save some for later!

What You'll Need:

4 chicken breasts (diced)
1 white onion
320g | 2 cups frozen peas
300g | 1 cup risotto rice
1 stock cube (chicken or veggie work best!)
1 tbsp. vegetable oil
1L | 1 quart boiling water

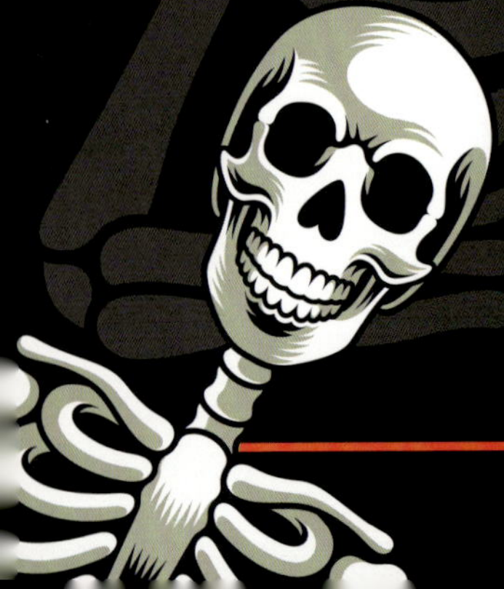

1. Add stock cubes to boiling water to dissolve.

2. Heat oil in a pan, and add chicken (cut into small strips), and diced onion and cook for 3 minutes, until browned. Add rice and stir, cooking for another minute.

3. Add your stock slowly, stirring and allowing the rice to absorb the stock before adding more. Continue until the rice is nearly cooked through (around 20 minutes).

4. Add the peas, a spoonful more of stock and salt and pepper to taste.

5. Once the rice is fully cooked and most of the stock is absorbed, this is ready to serve or stash for later!

This recipe makes 4 servings.

FISH FINGER
TACOS

This meal is a real catch when hosting guests!

What You'll Need:

8 fish fingers (frozen)
2 tbsp. mayonnaise
2 tbsp. sweet chilli sauce
4 mini tortillas
Cucumber (sliced)
Lettuce

Cook the fish fingers using instructions on the packet.

Mix mayonnaise and sweet chilli sauce together. Toast tortillas over medium-high heat in a pan.

Top the tortillas with fish fingers, lettuce and cucumber and drizzle with the sauce.

SAVE YOUR
PRODUCE

I know that you may have this idea that a lot of vegetables don't freeze well, and it's true that some veggies can go soft, soggy, and gross when they are defrosted. However, certain veg are great frozen, and can be used in cooking without taking away from their flavor and texture.

This means you can buy in bulk, pre-slice and chop to your desired shape, and freeze - ready to throw in to any dish (saving you loads of time too!)

The best for freezing are:

Sweetcorn (the kernels)
Carrots
Courgette (Zucchini)
Potato
Cauliflower
Broccoli
Kale
Onions

Essentially, any vegetable that doesn't have a high water content can be frozen and reused well, especially when cooking with it.

If you don't want to go through the hassle of dicing your own vegetables, you can now get pre-cut and pre-frozen vegetables in most stores. Just because you are eating food from the freezer, doesn't mean you can't still have your 5 a day!

THINGS YOU DIDN'T KNOW *YOU COULD* FREEZE

There are a lot of ingredients and food pantry staples that go bad easily, and can famously end up in the trash. This can be annoying, especially when those ingredients weren't cheap!

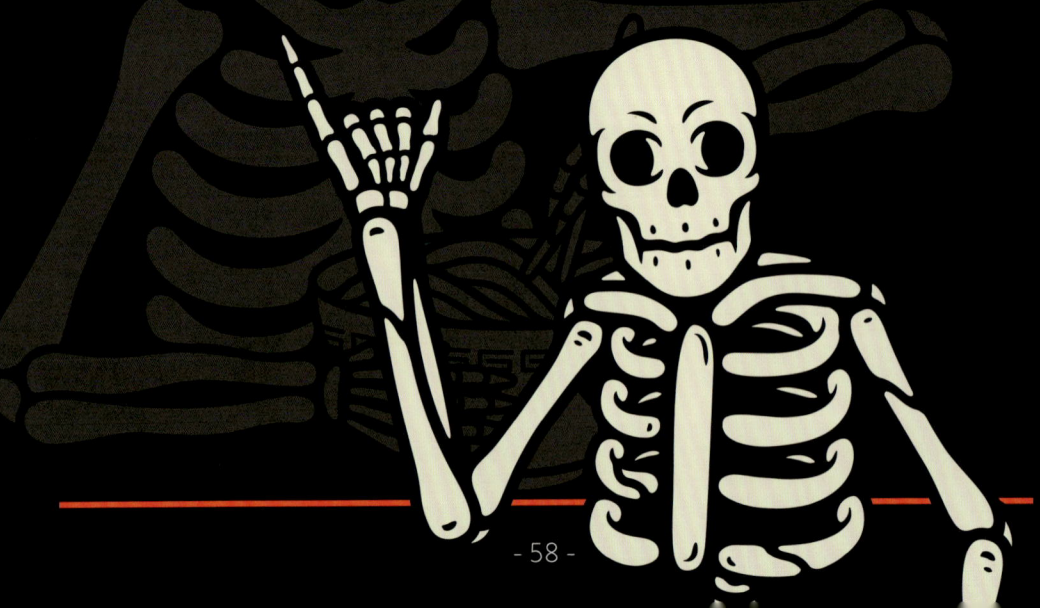

Did you know that your freezer can be the answer for some of these surprising ingredients:

Pesto - Pesto is expensive, and always seems to get mouldy quickly! Put spoonfuls of pesto in an ice cube tray and defrost for sandwiches, or drop straight into a hot pan for pasta and soups.

Shredded Cheese - Cheese also goes bad easily, but now there is no need to throw it in the trash. Buying blocks of cheese and grating it yourself, before freezing it, is a great way to preserve your cheese for cooking with, and saves you money.

Wine - Have you ever opened a bottle of wine, and not quite been able to finish the rest? (Crazy right?!) Well, pouring it into an ice cube tray and freezing the leftovers will stop it spoiling. These are great for cooking with, or for putting in a sangria or cocktail!

MEAL PREP
AND BULK
BUYING

One of the great ways to save yourself some dosh
(and time) is to cook in bulk and store it for later!
Realistically, it is just as much effort to cook one
portion as it is to cook 4, and cooking 4 means you
have three free dinners to redeem in future.

Ingredients are also much cheaper to buy in large quantities, but usually you won't want to in case they go bad or you don't have the space to. Here, your freezer will be your best friend. Meat is a lot cheaper in bulk packs, so buy, divide into individual portions and freeze! The same goes for seafood, herbs, sauces, stock and gravy!

If you usually find that you are too lazy to cook, as many of us can feel a lot of the time, just wait until you get a burst of energy, cook big portions of meals, divide into individual portions and freeze! Then, you can just defrost when you need it.

Not only have you saved money by buying large quantities of ingredients in one go, but you have also saved time - something your lazy self will thank you for when you just want to chill and eat (it could cut down those take-out bills too!)

LEFT OVERS

RECIPES AND HACKS

Have your bananas over-ripened? Maybe your bread has become stale, or you're left with extra food from the night before? Don't throw it all in the trash, save some cash and get cooking with these delicious and ingredient reviving meals!

CHOCOLATE AND BANANA
FRENCH TOAST

Has your bread gone stale but you need a breakfast pick me up after a few too many the night before?

Stale bread is actually great for soaking up flavors and retaining its structure (not going mushy) when introduced to moisture, making it a perfect ingredient for French toast.

Our recipe is for chocolate and banana but you could mix it up using whatever you have to hand!

What You'll Need:

**4 slices of stale white bread
3 medium eggs
1/8 cup | 25g unsalted butter
1 tbsp. cream
1 tbsp. maple syrup
1 tsp. vanilla extract
1 ripe banana
1/3 cup | 75g milk chocolate**

1. Mash your banana and mix with your chocolate in a bowl. Spoon the mixture evenly across two slices of bread. Top with your second slice of bread to make a sandwich.

2. Whisk together your eggs, cream, maple syrup and vanilla extract.

3. Melt the butter in a large frying pan, meanwhile lay 1 side of your sandwich into the egg mixture to coat it and repeat on the other side.

4. Once both sides of the sandwich are coated, lower carefully into your frying pan and cook for around 1 minute on each side until the bread becomes a golden brown and you can see that the chocolate has started to melt.

5. Repeat for the second sandwich and serve.

TATER
CAKES

Leftover mash makes a meal in a flash!

1. Add leftover mashed potatoes, shredded cheddar, flour, and 2 eggs into a bowl and stir well to make a soft, slightly sticky dough.

2. Scoop out balls of mixture and flatten them into thick circles.

3. Heat oil in a frying pan over medium heat. Place the potato cakes into the pan and cook for around 3-5 minutes (or until golden brown).

REHEATING
LEFTOVER
PIZZA

Take a slice out of yesterday's budget.

1. Heat a skillet over medium heat.

2. Add the pizza slices and cook for a couple of minutes, uncovered.

3. On the side of the pan (not on the pizza), add a few drops of water.

4. Immediately cover the pan with a lid and cook the pizza for a few more minutes, or until the cheese is melted and the pizza is heated through.

CROUTONS

Turn leftover, almost stale bread into croutons!

Do you ever find that bread just seems to go stale before you can use up the full loaf? Stale bread actually can be used and revived - our favorite thing to turn it into is some croutons!

Not only are these cheaper than buying them from a store, they can also stop food waste!

1. Chop or tear up your bread into bite-sized pieces.

2. Add to a bowl with some garlic powder, salt, pepper, and Italian herbs. Drizzle some oil over them and place in the oven at 180°C (356°F) until golden brown.

3. Store these for up to 1 week and add to your favorite salads!

BAKED
BANANA

Need a sweet treat but nothing but a ripe banana
and a few leftover chunks of chocolate in the fridge?

Turn the oven or air fryer on and get cracking with
this baked banana recipe.

What You'll Need:

1 ripe banana
32g | 1/5 cup chocolate chips

1. Make a cut down your banana through the skin.

2. Stuff your chocolate evenly through the slit.

3. Wrap your banana loosely in tin foil and add to a preheated oven.

4. Cook for 20-25 minutes until your banana has gone black.

5. Unwrap and enjoy!

Mix and match your chocolatey treats stuffed in your banana to what you have in or try with peanut butter!

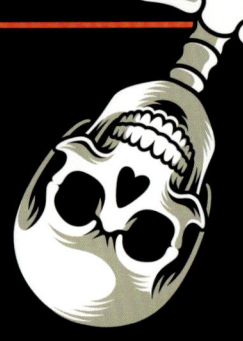

RICE
PUDDING

Turn last night's rice into something nice with this yummy dessert!

What You'll Need:

400g | 2 cups leftover plain rice (cooked)
475ml | 2 cups whole milk
4tbsp. sugar
1tsp. vanilla extract

Add rice, milk, sugar, and a pinch of salt into a large pan, and cook on medium heat for 20 minutes (or until thickened), stirring often.

Remove pan from the heat, and add vanilla essence, stirring well.

Serve while warm in a bowl, and enjoy!

Why not top with jam, whipped cream or a sprinkle of cinnamon for extra flavor?

CURRY
TOASTIE

Get creative with leftover curry!

1. Take a few slices of bread (we suggest 4), butter them, and spread your leftover curry generously over 2 slices.

2. Add some cheese over the curry.

3. Top with the remaining slices of bread, put under the grill.

4. Grill on medium-high heat for 3-4 minutes (or until golden brown in color).

Why not try adding a dollop of mango chutney on the side?

CHICKEN NOODLE SOUP

Had a roast chicken or perhaps just a bucket of chicken wings – whatever it may be, make sure to save your bones to turn into this delicious chicken noodle soup.

What You'll Need:

2 cup | 500ml chicken stock
1 ½ cup | 150g noodles of choice
½ red chili (sliced)
¼ Chinese cabbage (shredded)
2 spring onions (sliced)
1 tbsp. ginger (chopped)
1 tbsp. honey
2 tbsp. dark soy sauce

To first make your chicken stock, bring to the boil in a large saucepan your chicken carcass/bones in 2L of salted water with an onion, carrot, leek, celery, peppercorns & garlic clove. Once boiling simmer for 3 hours. Strain chicken stock through a sieve before using for your recipe.

1. Drizzle honey over the base of a large saucepan until it begins to bubble then add in the soy sauce, chilli, ginger and the chicken stock. Bring this to heat and let simmer for around 10 minutes, stirring intermittently.

2. Add your noodles and cabbage and cook for a further 5 minutes. The cabbage should have wilted and noodles should be heated through and soft.

3. Add the spring onions and serve!

FRIED RICE
ARANCINI

Never waste a single grain of rice again with this quick recipe!

What You'll Need:

Leftover fried rice (or any pre-cooked rice you have)
½ white onion (diced)
1 clove garlic (minced)
Parmesan (grated)
Cheddar cut into 1cm cubes
(or any white hard cheese you have in the refrigerator)
Plain flour
1 egg (beaten)
1 bag potato chips (crushed)

1. Put oil in a saucepan on medium heat. Add diced onion and garlic then fry for 5 minutes. Remove from the pan and add to the cold fried rice with some parmesan (make these as cheesy as you'd like!).

2. Mix well until sticky then divide the mixture, wrapping it around cubed cheese to make small balls 2cm wide. Roll the balls into flour, then beaten egg, and then crushed up potato chips.

3. Fry the balls at 170°C/340°F for 2-3 minutes (or until golden brown), then serve with a condiment of your choice!

CHEAP
BITES

At the end of the month, things can get a little tight when it comes to splurging out on a hearty meal... But you don't have to rob a bank to have a bite to eat! With these cheap and cheerful recipes, you can treat your tastebuds for a fraction of the cost!

HOMEMADE
PESTO

Pesto is delicious. We are all in agreement with that (unless you're a weirdo)... However, it is ALSO very expensive. Did you know that you can easily make your own fresh pesto, using a variety of ingredients that you might have in the refrigerator?

Pesto is technically any paste that is made by being pounded in a mortar and pestle, but you can add anything you like, and is a great way to use up greens and herbs that might be going off.

To make pesto, combine basil with some hard cheese, pine nuts, lemon juice, olive oil, salt and pepper! Feel free to swap out the pine nuts for any you have laying around (cashews and almonds work well)!

You can also throw in spinach, rocket (arugula) parsley and other ingredients you need to use! Just blend them together for a delicious sauce!

Get creative and make your own combos, and make in bulk and freeze! You'll be able to make delicious pesto for a fraction of the cost!

GOULASH

When it comes to the cost of ingredients, you can't go wrong with a bowl of goulash!

What You'll Need:

450g | 1lb ground beef
225g | 2 cups macaroni
1 bell pepper (diced)
1 can chopped tomatoes
100g | 1 cup cheese (grated)
1 tsp. basil
1 tsp. oregano
½ tsp. salt
½ tsp. pepper

1. Boil macaroni in a pan until soft, then drain the water and place back into the pan.

2. Cook the ground beef and peppers in a frying pan until the beef is browned.

3. Add tomatoes and seasoning into the meat, then add the macaroni and stir well.

4. Place into 4 bowls, then sprinkle cheese on top, before serving!

PIMP UP YOUR
INSTANT
RAMEN

Instant ramen is fine on its own, but sometimes you just need a little something extra to turn this snack into a meal. You should see ramen as a blank canvas, to experiment and turn them into a hearty meal.

What You'll Need:

1 packet instant ramen
½ tbsp. cooking oil
240g | 1 cup vegetable broth
1 garlic clove (minced)
½ tsp. fresh ginger (grated)
1 egg
Vegetables (mushrooms/ spinach)

In a small pan, add oil, ginger and garlic then sauté over medium heat for 1 minute. Add sliced mushrooms then heat for another minute.

Add the broth and 1 cup of water, then bring to a boil. Add the ramen and allow to boil for 3 minutes, then add spinach.

Turn to low heat, then crack an egg into the mixture and allow to sit for around 6 minutes (or unti egg whites are cooked).

Transfer the broth into a bowl, and enjoy!

BEAN
QUESADILLA

Bean quesadilla? No question!

1. Heat a can of your favorite beans (black beans or kidney beans work well) over a medium heat, adding some fajita seasoning to taste!

2. Dice up and throw in any leftover vegetables you have and add to the bean mixture. We recommend tomatoes, mushrooms, onion and bell peppers! Cook for 5 minutes and remove from the heat.

3. In a seperate frying pan, place a tortilla down and load up one half of it with your beany mixture.

4. Add cheese and some lettuce, and fold the tortilla in half!

5. Cook on both sides until golden brown and the cheese has melted. Serve with some sour cream or hot sauce and enjoy!

SPAGHETTI
AGLIO E OLIO

Who knew garlic and spaghetti could make a meal fit for a king?

What You'll Need:

200g | 7oz spaghetti
3 tbsp. extra virgin olive oil
4 garlic cloves (finely chopped)
½ red chili (finely chopped)
1 handful parsley (chopped)

1. Bring a pan of salted water to boil, then cook spaghetti for 10 minutes.

2. Heat oil in a frying pan on medium heat, then add chilli and garlic for 1 minute.

3. Drain the spaghetti and add to the frying pan with parsley. Stir well, then serve!

TORTILLA
PIZZA

Pizza on a budget? Yes please!

What You'll Need:

4 tbsp. tomato purée
1 garlic clove (crushed)
½ tbsp. olive oil
½ tsp. dried herbs
2 tortillas
50g | ½ cup mozzarella (grated)
Pepperoni slices
Pickled jalapeños

1. Preheat oven to 220°C/ 425°F, and place tortillas onto a baking sheet.

2. Mix tomato purée, olive oil, garlic and herbs well, then spread evenly around the tortillas, leaving a small border around the edges.

3. Scatter mozerella evenly onto both tortillas, and top with pepperoni and jalapenos.

4. Bake in the oven for 6 minutes or until the tortillas are golden around the edges.

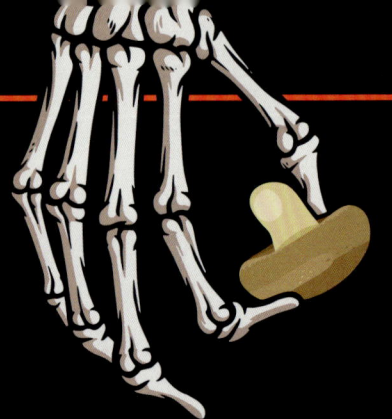

CHESTNUT
MUSHROOM
RAGU

What You'll Need:

2 onions (finely diced)
4 garlic cloves (crushed)
2 celery stalks (finely diced)
316g | 2 cups chestnut mushrooms (finely minced)
100ml | ½ cup dry sherry
1 tbsp. tomato purée
200ml | 1 cup vegetable stock
2 tbsp. butter

In a large pan, add the garlic, celery and onions in a little olive oil. When they become soft (and onions are translucent), turn up the heat then add mushrooms, frying until golden.

Add sherry and stir well, then add the other ingredients. Allow to cook for 1 hour, then enjoy!

Why not serve alongside your favorite pasta?

INSTANT RICE
REMASTERED

Cheap meal in an instant? Spam can!

What You'll Need:

1 can of Spam
3 eggs (beaten)
3 packs instant microwavable rice
100g | ½ cup frozen peas
100g | ½ cup frozen sweetcorn
2 green onions (chopped)
2 garlic cloves (minced)
4 tbsp. soy sauce

1. Add 1 tbsp. oil into a skillet and heat over medium-high heat. Add the eggs and stir until half cooked, then place onto a plate.

2. Add another 1 tbsp. oil to the pan and fry spam pieces for 2 minutes (until crisp and browned). Add garlic and onion and fry for 1 minute.

3. Add corn and peas and fry for 30 seconds, then add rice and toss until mixed. Add soy sauce and egg then heat through.

This recipe makes 4 servings.

SPICY
STIR FRY

Don't cry, make a stir fry!

500g | 1.1lbs pork mince
3 spring onions (sliced)
250g | 2 cups green beans (sliced)
2 deseeded chilis (sliced)
2 garlic cloves (crushed)
1 tbsp. ginger (chopped)
2 tsp. brown sugar
2 tbsp. soy sauce
2 tbsp. oyster sauce

1. Heat oil over high heat in a pan. Once hot, add garlic, chilli, ginger, and spring onions, then stir well, and cook for a minute.

2. Add the mince, and cook through. add green beans and stir fry, then add sugar, soy sauce, oyster sauce, and 2 tbsp. water.

3. Cook for 2 minutes, then serve with your favourite noodles or rice!

FAKEAWAY
RECIPES

Fancy a takeout but don't have the cash? Don't wither away while dreaming of your favorite fried chicken or burger meal... make it yourself!

These fakeaway recipes are perfect for satisfying your cravings, without burning a hole in your wallet!

SMASH *BURGERS*

Hungry? Why not smash together a few burgers?

What You'll Need:

2 burger buns (of your choice)
½ tbsp. sunflower oil
250g | 8oz steak mince
Mild cheddar (2 slices)
1 red onion (sliced)
Iceburg lettuce
1 tomato (sliced)
1 gherkin

1. Half your burger buns then toast lightly.

2. Heat ¼ tbsp. oil on high heat in a frying pan.

3. Divide mince into 2 piles and season with salt, then place one pile into the pan

4. Cover with baking paper and press the mince down hard using a smaller pan.

5. Allow to cook for 2 minutes then turn the patty over, and press down with a spatula. Add a slice of cheese and allow to cook for another minute.

6. Do the same again to cook the other patty.

7. Assemble the burger in your preferred order, then eat up!

8. Why not add your favorite sauces to the mix?

HOMEMADE
BHAJIS

Delicious onion bhajis?
Promise not to make you cry!

What You'll Need:

2 onions (sliced)
100g | ½ cups gram flour
½ tsp. baking powder
½ tsp. chilli powder
½ tsp. turmeric
1 green chili (finely chopped, deseeded)
Vegetable oil

1. Soak onion in cold water.

2. In a bowl, sift flour and baking powder, then add tumeric, chili powder, a sprinkle of salt and chopped chili.

3. Mix 100ml/3.4oz cold water to the mix to create a thick batter. Drain the onion well and add to the batter.

4. Add oil to a wok (no more than ⅓ full) and heat up. Using a tablespoon, lower a few scoops bhaji mix into the pan and cook until crisp and brown.

HOMEMADE COLONEL
FRIED CHICKEN

For a finger lickin' good meal for a fraction of the cost, look no further than this foolproof fakeaway!

What You'll Need:

4 chicken drumsticks (or cut of your choice)
400g | 2 cups flour
¼ tbsp. garlic salt
½ tbsp. paprika
½ tsp. each - dried thyme, ginger, basil, white pepper, black pepper, salt, celery salt, dry mustard
½ tsp. dried oregano
300ml | 1 ¼ cups buttermilk

1. In a bowl, mix buttermilk, ¼ tbsp. paprika, ½ tsp. garlic salt, ¼ tsp. dried oregano, thyme, ginger, basil, celery salt, black and white pepper, salt, and mustard.

2. Place all 4 chicken drumsticks into the mixture and coat well, then leave in the fridge for 24 hours to marinate.

3. Add the rest of the ingredients into a bowl and mix well, then coat the chicken drumsticks thoroughly.

4. Heat oil in a pan, and fry chicken for 8 minutes, removing excess oil with a kitchen towel.

HOMEMADE
BIG McSTACK

To make this iconic staple in fast-food history, first, you're going to need to make the iconic sauce!

Simply mix together the following ingredients:
225g | 1 cup mayonnaise
2 tbsp. India relish (drained)
½ tsp. granulated sugar
½ tbsp. thousand island dressing

For the burgers, you'll need:
680g | 1 ½ lb ground chuck
5 burger buns
(Plus 5 extra bottom halves for the center)
5 tbsp. onion (minced)
1 tbsp. butter
American cheese (5 slices)
Dill pickles (sliced)
Lettuce

1. Add the ground beef into a bowl then season with salt and pepper. Divide the meat into 10 equal pieces, then flatten into thin patties.

2. Heat a griddle pan to 177°C / 350°F, then place the patties into the pan and cook for 6-8 minutes (or until juices run clear), flipping halfway.

3. Spead butter over the bread buns, and place into the pan to lightly toast.

4. Assemble the burgers in this order:
    Bottom bun, sauce, onions, lettuce, cheese, burger, middle bun, sauce, onions, lettuce, burger, 3 pickles, top bun.

BLACK BEAN
CHOW MEIN

Visit the Great Wall of cheap with this iconic Chinese recipe!

What You'll Need:

300g | 11oz beef rump steak (sliced into strips)
40ml | 1⅓oz groundnut oil
250g | 9oz egg noodles
3 spring onions (sliced)
1 onion (chopped)
1 tsp. cornflour
1 tsp. caster sugar
2 tbsp. soy sauce
Stir fry sauce

1. In a bowl, whisk soy sauce, sugar and cornflour together. Add the beef and coat evenly with the mixture.

2. Blanch egg noodles in a boiling saucepan for 3-4 minutes, then add to cold water.

3. Over medium heat, add groundnut oil to a wok until hot, then stir-fry onion and spring onion, before adding the beef, then cook for 2-3 minutes, stirring frequently.

4. Drain the noodles, then add into the wok along with the stir fry sauce, and continue to stir for 2 minutes.

5. Serve, and enjoy!

CAULIFLOWER
BIRYANI

This cost-cutting cauliflower biryani will bring the taste of Asia to your palate!

What You'll Need:

1 cauliflower (cut into small florets)
1 red onion (diced)
160g | 1¼ cups green beans (sliced)
1 tbsp. tomato paste
1 tbsp. curry powder
130g | ¾ cup basmati rice
30g | 1oz sultanas
2 tbsp. vegetable stock

1. In a large pan, heat 2 tbsp. vegetable oil over high heat. Once hot, add onion, cauliflower, curry powder and a pinch of salt and pepper (to taste), then cook for 5 minutes.

2. Add tomato paste and vegetable stock to the pan and cook for another 2 minutes, then add contents to a bowl.

3. In the pan, add rice and 350ml | 1 ½ cups water and allow to boil on high heat. Add the cauliflower mixture to the pan and add green beans and sultanas.

4. Reduce to medium-low heat, cover, and cook for 10 minutes (or until water has been absorbed).

PRAWN
TOAST

What You'll Need:

200g | 7oz raw and peeled prawns (or shrimp)
1 garlic clove (chopped)
1 egg white
2 spring onions (finely chopped)
3 slices white bread (crusts removed)
1 tsp. ginger (finely grated)
½ tsp. golden caster sugar
1 tsp. soy sauce
1 egg (beaten)
100g | 3.5oz sesame seeds
Sesame oil
Sunflower oil

1. Blitz prawns, egg white, garlic, ginger, soy sauce, and sugar in a food processor until a paste is made. Add spring onion, stir, then chill in the fridge for 30 minutes.

2. One one side of the bread, brush lightly with sesame oil then add the prawn mix on top, smoothing to the edges of the bread. Brush beaten egg over the top and sides then cover well with sesame seeds.

3. Heat some sunflower oil in a frying pan then cook the bread spread-side up for 1 ½ minutes, before flipping and cooking for another 2 minutes.

4. Serve with soy sauce for dipping!

HINTS AND TIPS

KITCHEN
DON'TS

Never reheat rice twice! Once rice has been reheated once, it's no longer safe to reheat again.

-

Don't cut into meat straight after removing from the grill - instead, let it sit a while, and it'll keep the juices within the meat!

-

Don't skip on preheating your cooker - you should wait a little while after your oven indicates it's at correct temperature, to be sure that it is truly at temperature and to compensate for any heat lost when opening the door.

RESTORING
FOOD

Don't worry if you've oversalted your food, just add a dash of vinegar, lemon juice, or brown sugar and the flavor will balance out!

-

Putting a little lemon juice on the brown parts of your veggies will slow down the spread!

-

Soft fruits and berries make for a great smoothie! Just blend them up with milk.

If your veggies are getting soft, soak them in ice water for 5 minutes, to bring back their original crisp texture.

-

Blend leftover or stale bread into soup and sauces to thicken them up.

-

Overcooked veggies can be pureed and turned into a sauce.
(Just add milk, vegetable stock, or cream to thicken it up!)

-

Keep your brown sugar fluffy (and avoid clumping) by adding some citrus peel in the container.

MAKE THE
SWITCH!

This might seem like a weird bit of advice, especially when thinking how to cut costs, but trust us - investing in the right appliances can massively help you in the long run to save money, time, and make your dishes delicious!

A quality air fryer can help you cut down your gas and electric costs, and is easy to make super delicious and effective dishes! A good slow cooker is also a great way to easily cook delicious curries, stews and soups whilst keeping your wallet happy!

KEY STAPLES FOR YOUR CUPBOARD

One way to level up your cooking is by having a good selection of herbs and spices to help give your meals that extra edge! A lot of this would depend on what kinds of food you prefer to prepare. However, some are far more versatile than others! Our staples would be:

Salt
Pepper
Italian Seasoning
Onion Powder
Garlic Powder
Smoked Paprika
Chili Powder (or Cayenne Pepper)
Crushed Chili Flakes
Ground Cinnamon
Ground Turmeric
Ground Cumin
Ground Coriander
Ground Ginger

Just these 13 spices are a great start to build up your pantry, and will go a long way with almost all dishes.

MIX UP
YOUR MEAT

Meat is expensive, and we can definitely feel the sting when buying cuts of it from the store. However, there are ways to save your pennies whilst still getting your protein!

Try to experiment with cheaper cuts of meat - these can be just as good (if not better) as the pricier options! Swapping chicken breast for the more flavorful and tender thigh meat is a great start. Lamb neck is a great alternative to lamb chops, and if cooked well, can be extremely tender. Pork collar is also a great alternative for shoulder!

You could also ask yourself if you need meat - could this be swapped for mushrooms, tofu or grains to help keep your costs low? Just remember - you don't need to blow your budget to blow your tastebuds away!

CUT THE COSTS!

There are many ways you can help to keep costs down in the kitchen, and most of these involve spending an extra 5 minutes prepping instead of cutting corners with ingredients.

Buy blocks of cheese and shred them yourself.
Dice your own garlic.
Mince your own ginger.
Buy whole vegetables and cut them down yourself.

This goes for other pre-prepared ingredients. When you are in the store, stop and think, could you do that yourself to save money?

STOP THE
SPOIL

By hanging up your fruit, you can delay them from spoiling and stop them bruising easily! Furthermore, if you keep your bananas away from other fruit, it will keep them fresher.

-

Keep fresh herbs (such as basil and parsley) fresher for longer by snipping the ends and adding them to the fridge, stood in a glass container with a little water in the bottom.

Glass containers with a sealable lid are much better at keeping food fresh than plastic containers, and most can be popped into the fridge or microwave. (win win!)

-

To make onions almost invincible, hang them in a pair of tights... you read right! Placing them in thin tights and tieing a knot between them can make them last up to 8 months longer!

-

Washing your berries in a vinegar solution can make them last up to 2 weeks longer - just mix 1 part distilled vinegar with 10 parts water.

-

Let your cheese breathe by wrapping in cheese or parchment paper rather than plastic, and thank us later!

After washing lettuce, add a paper towel to the container to soak up any moisture to stop it wilting quickly.

-

Storing mushrooms in a paper bag can keep them from spoiling as it won't trap moisture.

-

Storing root vegetables in a pot full of sand in a dark and cool area will keep them fresher for much longer!